Foxes

Dexter Flanders

Author's Note

Foxes was due to go into rehearsals one week
before the first UK lockdown in March 2020.

After many drafts and workshops this piece was ready for
the actors to dissect before getting it on its feet. Small
changes are to be made during the rehearsal process.

methuen | drama

LONDON • NEW YORK • OXFORD • NEW DELHI • SYDNEY

METHUEN DRAMA
Bloomsbury Publishing Plc
50 Bedford Square, London, WC1B 3DP, UK
1385 Broadway, New York, NY 10018, USA
29 Earlsfort Terrace, Dublin 2, Ireland

BLOOMSBURY, METHUEN DRAMA and the Methuen
Drama logo are trademarks of Bloomsbury Publishing Plc

First published in Great Britain 2021

A catalogue record for this book is available from the British Library.

ISBN: PB: 978-1-3501-8395-7
ePDF: 978-1-3501-8396-4
eBook: 978-1-3501-8397-1

Series: Modern Plays

Typeset by Mark Heslington Ltd, Scarborough, North Yorkshire

To find out more about our authors and books visit
www.bloomsbury.com and sign up for our newsletters.

Foxes

For Anthony, Joanna and Augustine

Our lives begin to
end the day we become silent about the
things that matter.
                    – Martin Luther King Jr

Characters

Daniel, *Black British, London mid-20s*
Leon, *Black British, London mid-20s*
Meera, *British Iranian, Birmingham. early 20s*
Deena, *Black British, London 19*
Patricia, *Black Jamaican, late 50s.*

The play is set in London 2020

Glossary

Say less/Say no more
Boda/Bother
Bruda/Brother
Certi/Certified
P/Money
Dun kno/No doubt
Peak/Bad luck
Pattern/Organise
Rasclat-Bludclat/Jamaican expletive
Yute/Youth
Tapped/Crazy
Packs/Drugs

A forward slash / indicates overlapping dialogue

Act One

Scene One

January. A winter evening. **Daniel** *and* **Meera** *stood in Clissold Park. A moment and then . . .*

Daniel   Are you sure?

Meera   Yes!

Pause.

Daniel   How many times did you check it?

Meera   I bought three of them!

Pause.

Daniel   Definitely mine, yeah?

Meera   Daniel don't take the piss.

Daniel   I'm just asking. Fucking hell man.

Look, now ain't the right / time for this, babe.

Meera   I know, I didn't plan for this to happen, did I?!

Beat.

Look, I'm not getting rid of it.

Daniel   Hold on, we haven't even spoke / about it.

Meera   We're speaking about it now.

Daniel   I know!

Meera   Look, there ain't gonna be no conversation where you convince me otherwise.

Scene Two

Daniel's *dreaming. He's in a big black cave. Hands and feet chained. He's stood star-shaped covered in tar, wearing only rags as underwear. Thunder and lightning roar through the sky. In front of him lies a baby wrapped up in a cot crying. The crying gets louder and louder.* **Daniel** *is petrified. He attempts to break free from the chains to help but can't.*

Fade to black.

Scene Three

Early morning. Living room. The room is open-plan with the kitchen. The flat is tidy and has 90s décor throughout. There is an assortment of odd chairs around a dinner table. A long sofa to the right. Opposite is a television and full-length mirror next to a cabinet full of books and old mail. **Patricia**, *whilst singing is getting ready for church.* **Deena** *enters doing her hair, stood in front the mirror.*

Patricia   I'm gonna laydown my burdens, down by di riverside, down by di riverside, down by di riverside. Daniel! – I'm gonna lay down my burdens, down by the river – Daniel! Dan –

Deena   He's got his headphones on.

Patricia   Mi na interested inna no headphones, dear. What mi want fi know is has he wash he skin . . .

Deena (*laughs*)   He had his towel in his hand.

Patricia   Hm!

Deena   You staying for the evening service, Mum?

Patricia   No darling, mi want fi get back to finish off dis job application, di deadline is tonight. Mi need to leave dis blasted job as soon as possible, yuh know di manager fi start call me Pat again?

Deena   Oh Mum!

Patricia (*mocking*) 'Pat love can you bring the invoices over', 'Pat love would you like a cup of tea' even after me tell di woman already, my muddah name me Patricia, mi look like a postman to yuh? Dis people make mi sick – Daniel!

Deena   I'll help you finish it if you want?

Patricia   Thank yuh dear, I just have di work experience and qualifications section fi fill out, that's di part which confuse mi brain di most. How deh expect mi fi remember every qualification and job I've had inna mi fifty-six years of life?

Deena   You just put the parts relative to the job.

Beat.

When's Meera moving in?

Patricia   Some of her things are already upstairs. She's gone to try and get di last of her stuff this marnin – Daniel nah make me fi call out your name again, boy!

Deena   Oh, Mum listen, you know Gemma downstairs?

Patricia   Uh hm.

Deena   You don't even know who I'm talking about, do you?

Patricia   Yes love, yuh friend with di tight up / tight up clothes.

Deena   No, that's Jasmin. I mean at number thirty-four . . . her mum works in the NatWest.

Patricia   Oh yes.

Deena   Anyway, her brother works for J.P. Morgan. I've got an interview next week for their junior analyst program. I'm trying to go in and smash this one. I need this right now.

Patricia   Mi so proud of yuh and di way yuh speak.

Deena   What do you mean?

Patricia   Just full of confidence.

Deena   You got to create your own opportunities out here right?

Patricia   Eh eh! Ah where yuh learn dat, yuh fada?

Deena   Yep – and TED talks n' dat . . . how often do you think of him?

Patricia   Every day.

Deena   Me too! I hear him saying Deena you are the architect of your own future, don't let nobody put their hands on you, and no matter what their job or status /(*In unison.*) everybody deserves respect!

Patricia   Everyone deserves your respect! (*Laughs.*) Pass me di brush pon di table – ah what di – Dan

Daniel *enters.*

Daniel   Yes Mum!

Patricia   Yuh backside been inna di bawtroom?

Daniel   Yep, but my back's killing me . . .

Deena   This guy!

Patricia   Na bother wid yuh nonsense, boy! Yuh back, yuh foot or whatever else yuh got paining yuh, yuh better put on some Bengay and get dressed because yuh na getting outta going church dis marnin, yuh hear me!

Deena *laughs.*

Daniel   What are you laughing at?

Deena   You! You ain't got no imagination, boy.

Daniel   Nah seriously, I injured it at football yesterday, my back's doing a madness right now.

Deena   Shut up!

Patricia   Put on yuh clothes and get ready, Daniel.

Daniel   I ain't going. Pastor Edwards is long anyway, always asking me if I'm coming mid-week mass, I feel pressured.

Deena   Don't we all . . .

Daniel   Yeah but he ain't onto you like that. I just wanna go when I wanna go rather than feel / guilty if I don't.

Patricia   I said Daniel get ready!

Deena   You know why we go. Every week you have some dead story to why you can't or don't want to come, but you're quick to go football or Nando's though, innit.

Patricia   That's enough Deena, finish getting ready upstairs.

Deena *goes.*

(*Beat.*) What's going on?

Daniel   What do you mean . . .

Patricia   Daniel, nuh boda play di fool wid me, Deena's right. Yuh been making all kinds of excuses and mi know yuh have a lot going on so mi never boda fi pressure you. Now yuh know yuh can always tell me anything, Daniel . . . so . . . I'm asking what's going on?

Daniel   I dunno . . . it's just . . . everything seems to be going so fast.

Patricia   Yuh fada woulda wanted yuh fi come, but just like him nobody was going mek im do anything im nuh waan do.

Daniel, do what yuh have to do to get yourself right. God understands, yuh hear me. You're taking care of your responsibilities and that's all I care about.

Daniel *nods in agreement.*

Patricia (*calling up*)   Deena, we're going!

Deena   But he's not / even . . .

Patricia   Just come downstairs young lady. Finish up the chicken yuh hear?

Daniel   Yes Mum.

Deena *enters.*

Patricia   Come Deena, your brother's back is playing up.

Deena   Golden boy, of course it is.

Patricia *and* **Deena** *leave.* **Daniel** *goes upstairs.*

Deena   Bare special treatment every time man.

Patricia   Stop yuh noise, child.

Scene Four

Daniel*'s living room. Afternoon.* **Daniel** *and* **Leon** *are blasting Drake feat Giggs 'KMT'. The two have deodorant cans as mics and are pretending to be on stage.* **Leon** *is dressed in football training gear and* **Daniel** *in comfy home clothes. They alternate the lines of the last verse of the song.*

Daniel   Jeeeeez, not gonna lie, dat verse is mad still!

Leon   Giggs ting pattern up nice.

Daniel   Every time man hears that, I wanna violate a man ya nah.

Leon   What?

Daniel   I don't mean like violate a bruda for no reason or nuttin. I mean like go mad on some mosh pit typa ting.

Leon   Say less! Oi, Reading festival yeah, man pulled up dat ting three times ya nah, ting was mad!

Daniel   Man needs to reach next year still.

Leon   What, wid a new born, yeah?

Daniel   Dickhead!

Leon   That's kinda mad still, man's gonna be a daddy n' shit.

Daniel   I know.

Leon (*beat*)   She just dropped it on man like that, yeah?

Daniel   Yeah, fam.

Leon (*beat*)   I can't imagine you being a dad.

Daniel   Yeah me / neither.

Leon   I mean, you can barely look after yourself.

Daniel   Shut up.

Leon   I watched you dip a custard cream in your coke and I thought . . . rah childish.

Daniel   Fool, man's *been* doing that.

Leon   Again . . . childish.

Daniel   Nah nah, it's calm. I just got to work out how I'm gonna do Uni and work.

Leon (*beat*)   Man could go back on road –

Daniel   No!

Leon   Cool . . . Take a year out?

Daniel   Are you mad! My mum will start drawing samurai swords cuz . . . anyway I'm in a routine / I'm organised now.

Leon   Yeah but your routine ain't gonna be the same for the next year anyway.

Daniel   Why you gotta be negative?

Leon   I'm being realistic my bruda.

Daniel   Well, go and be realistic somewhere else.

Leon   You told me to holla *you*.

Daniel   Cool, well just allow man for a sec then, innit.

Leon   Normal.

Beat.

Shit! I got a new ting for you yeah, would you rather drink . . .

Daniel   It's long, I'm not on it.

Leon   Shut up before I forget it . . . would you rather – and remember this is to save your mum's life, innit – drink a pint of Beyoncé's sweat or saliva?

Daniel   Nah bro . . .

Leon   Come on, answer the ting man.

Daniel   Err, ah bro!

Leon   It's a mad, innit.

Daniel   Nahhh . . .

Leon   Come on man!

Pause.

Well!

Daniel   Shh, I'm thinking . . .

Leon (*laughs*)   Ahh it's peak, innit.

Daniel   Man's going with the saliva.

Leon   Saliva that's half Jay Z's, yeah?

Daniel   What? You going with the sweat?

Leon   Fam, don't ask big man questions, this questions for you, innit. Man wouldn't get himself into them kinda predicaments in the first place you get me . . .

Daniel   Pagan!

Leon (*beat*)   Meera's family's pissed?

Daniel *nods.*

Leon   Yeah, Islam ain't playing, bro.

Daniel   Her pap's kicked her out the same day, ya nah.

Leon   Nah, man's tapped still.

Daniel   Come on.

Leon   What's your mum saying?

Daniel   Just take care of my responsibilities and she'll support me.

Leon   Yo, your mum's certi.

Daniel   Dun know! You know the maddest ting . . . is man had his life all planned out and now man's gonna have to look after another actual human being, bro . . .

Leon   I feel you. Well put it like this, you see my first carer yeah . . . he said when he first found he was gonna be a dad n' that, his head was all over the place – not saying you're all over the place so relax – but shortly after he said it gave him focus. Man's work ethic changed because man knew he couldn't allow no fatherless child to wander into the world like he did. So, it's how you respond to things that define you my bruda, you feel me?

Knocking at the front door.

Leon   I'll get it, I'll get it – you get what I'm saying though, innit. Look, if you need anything I got you anyway.

Knocking at the front door again.

Leon   Hello!

Deena   Yeah, it's me.

Leon   Who's me?

Deena (*banging door*)   Quick it's cold outside, man.

Leon *opens the door.*

Leon   Where's your keys?

Deena   Shut up . . . move man you don't even live here. Why you always here, go do suttin man.

Deena *enters approaching* **Daniel**. **Deena** *pulls out a selection of baby clothing*.

Deena   Look what I got.

Daniel   Why you getting excited for, you don't even know if it's a girl . . .

Deena   Firstly, your child is not an IT, also these are unisex.

Look how cute these are though.

She then pulls out baby Nike trainers.

I got these also. I'll keep these under my bed anyway, tell Meera where they are. Where's Mum?

Daniel   Still at work.

Leon*'s been staring at* **Deena**.

Deena   Cool. (*To* **Leon**.) Are you alright? What you looking at?

Leon (*mocking*)   Are you alright. What you looking at?

Deena   You think you live here innit, opening doors like you pay rent n' shit, and take your dusty beat down hat off the table before my mum comes back.

Leon *doesn't move.*

Daniel   What's work saying?

Deena   Dead, they tried to make me supervisor today. You know when they can low key tell you're trying to leave innit, they start offering out positions n' shit but I'm like you can miss me wid that. I got a second interview with this J.P. Morgan ting, so we'll see hopefully.

Daniel   Second interview and dat yeah, come on D.

Deena   Right, let me sort these bags out, in a bit.

Deena *goes.*

Leon   One of these days I'm gonna beat up your sister
you know.

So you definitely ain't coming training, nah?

Daniel *doesn't respond.*

(*Beat.*) Yo! You alive?

Daniel   Just daydreaming.

Leon   Them ones. Right my guy, I'll tell them you're sick
again, that's why you ain't coming training, yeah?

Daniel   I text Terry already.

Leon   Alright cool. I know you don't wanna see no one
but football will clear your mind you know, cuz . . . bro you
bless, yeah?

Daniel   Yeah yeah, holla me later, innit.

Leon   Say nuttin.

Leon *goes.*

Scene Five

Living room. Morning. **Deena** *is busily searching for her brush.*

Deena   You can't find nuttin in dis house you know . . .
Mum . . . Mum . . . Mu!

Patricia *exits the toilet.*

Deena   Oh, thought you were upstairs. have you seen my –

Patricia   Whose hat is that pon mi table?

Deena   Ah Leon's, I told him last night to –

Patricia   Tell Daniel fi tell im friend this is not a hotel. Bwoy
come like him live here.

Deena   That's exactly what I told him. Have you seen
my brush?

Patricia   I give it to Meera fi use quickly.

Deena   Ah Mum!

Patricia   She hasn't got all her stuff here – stop yuh noise, child!

Meera *enters giving* **Deena** *her brush.*

Meera   Deena.

Deena *takes her brush.* **Meera** *sits.*

Deena   Ah, nah you can use it, I was / just saying.

Meera   No, it's fine, I'm done. Don't worry about it, I'm the same with my stuff.

Deena   Mum I need to talk to you about something.

Patricia   When?

Deena   Right now.

Patricia   No darling, not right now, I'm running behind already, we'll catch up later alright. Turn off di hot water before yuh leave out. Meera, help yourself to what you need, there's all kinda food in there darling, alright.

Meera   Thank you. You still good for four then?

Patricia   Yes, meet mi outside di post office.

Deena   Where you two going?

Patricia   I just waan show her a couple things to pick up that will be useful for di baby. I see you at four.

Meera   Thanks, Patricia.

Patricia   Deena, have a good day.

Patricia *goes.*

Deena   I was being selfish, use whatever you need.

Meera   Thanks.

Deena (*beat*)   Meera.

Pause.

Meera

Pause.

Deena (*leaving*)   Anyway, if you wanna to talk I'm here –

Meera   Thankless child . . . he kicked over the table and screamed 'thankless child'. I never heard my dad scream like that before . . . ever. He never even raises his voice. I mean I've heard him scream you know, at the TV, but there was something about the quality. I knew he meant it. He didn't even want to hear me out. He just kept repeating 'this will bring shame on the family if you keep it, this will bring shame on the family if you keep it'. Mum just stood there, staring at me or through me, I couldn't quite tell. You hear about this happening in my community but when it's you you're like, how the hell am I in this situation. Five minutes it took for them to disown me. All I could think was 'Allah has blessed me with a child, Allah has blessed me with a child' over and over. He quotes the Quran and Hadiths at me like he wrote them sometimes, yet the moment a real-life situation arose he saw abortion as an instant option to save face and embarrassment. Deena, have I been living a lie, is the use of Scripture for show? Because I know in my heart Allah isn't going to give me anything I can't deal with. So, he's going to have to take a pew and relax on this one because I'm going to be a mum . . . and that's a beautiful thing . . . right?

Deena   Right.

Meera   Sorry for chewing your ear off.

Deena   Don't be silly, that's what I'm here for. I know what it's like to feel like you're not being heard.

Meera   Yeah?

Deena   Yep. Sometimes I'm like, is anybody even listening? It's weird how you can feel so alone in a house full of people. Since my dad passed I feel that often, man. He would sit there eating Twiglets, swigging super malt and stare at me and listen . . . never interrupting . . . just listening to me rant about anything and everything. He used to say 'if we all brought our problems to the centre of the world, we would gladly take our own back home rather than take a portion of the common stock' . . . and when life's quiet I'm like . . . that so true . . .

Meera   He sounds like a great man . . . also seems you're a good listener like he was.

Deena   Well, I don't know about all that, try telling that to my mum. Listen, you have a place here with us, OK? Right I've got to go.

Meera   OK, I better get on with some work.

Beat.

You got your head screwed on, haven't you . . .

Deena   Lord knows I'm trying . . . see you later.

Scene Six

Living room. Early afternoon.

Meera   You're back early.

Daniel   Yeah, couldn't really focus . . . bare questions every minute, 'You gonna be a dad', 'What's Meera's family saying . . .'

Meera   And what do you say?

Daniel   What?

Meera   When they ask you?

Daniel   What do you mean?

Meera   Daniel!

Daniel   Nothing! I just wanna focus on my work. End of the day it's none of anyone's business but our's right.

Meera   Exactly –

Daniel   There we go.

Beat.

I'm just adjusting, that's all. Ain't been sleeping properly and I'm having some mad dreams but look, I'm here and ready to do what needs to
be done.

Meera   Fuck, you sound like some politician.

Beat.

Look, I want to be here with you as long as you want / me to
be –

Daniel   And I do, sorry if it's coming across that way. I love you, like I said I'm just adjusting that's all.

Daniel *pulls a piece paper out his pocket.*

Look at this, I booked these parenting classes for us to go on.

Meera   I'm not going to a class.

Daniel   Why not?

Meera   Because there's no manual on how to raise a child, our parents didn't have one.

Daniel   And look how that turned out . . . I'm joking, but let's just go anyway. I've paid already, so we can go check it out and if we like it go again or if we find we wanna kill ourselves then fuck 'em.

Meera   Sure, babe.

Daniel   Cool.

Meera (*beat*)   What do you think about God?

Daniel   Huh, where did that come from?

Meera   I'm halfway through my module on the origins of religions and was thinking, I wonder what Daniel thinks. I know you ain't really feeling the church thing at the mo . . . so . . .

Daniel   I don't chat about dat, Meera!

Meera   I'm curious!

Pause.

Daniel   OK . . . so what do I think about God? I dunno . . . I believe in him.

Meera   And?

Daniel (*beat*)   OK, this might sound Btec, yeah.

Meera   Daniel.

Daniel   I dunno . . . but I always had a sense there was something, you get me, and got introduced to God, Jesus n' dat. As I got older I started to have more questions. Like it played on my mind that I basically wasn't practicing anything from the Bible, even though man was at church every week. I felt guilty, which actually just moved me away from God, because I thought how can man sit here go church and pray when I'm doing bare madness. Also, I thought like if I was born in India, Iran or in some remote part of Australia, would I have a different belief, meaning is my belief purely geographical? I still believe in God and Jesus but also think whether you call it God, Allah, Krishna or high power – or whatever, that that's just language and ultimately if we have love, care, forgiveness and tolerance then we are all basically saying the same thing, you feel me babes? Apart from that I mind my own rasclat business to what others are doing. The End.

Meera *laughs.*

Meera   I like it.

Beat.

Doesn't sound Btec at all. You're so different from when we first met. You thought you was a bad man, innit?

Daniel   Man is bad man, babes.

Meera   Yeah, of course you are. Who do you live with again? I'm not trying to embarrass you. I think it's sweet.

Daniel *goes to tickle* **Meera**.

Daniel   Man's only sweet on you, babes.

Meera   Get off. How long do you think I can stay here for?

Daniel   As long as you want, why?

Meera   I can't stay here as long as I want, Daniel.

Daniel   Why not?

Meera   This isn't my home.

Daniel   Course it is. Look, my mum said you can and if she says that then she means it because she ain't never told anyone they can stay here, let alone for as long they want.

Meera   OK. Thanks babe.

Daniel   You heard anything from home?

Meera   I tried my dad, still won't pick up . . . also according to Sandra next door, apparently he's changed the locks.

Daniel   Nah, there's levels, man, that's some extreme shit.

Meera   Yeah but what can I do.

Daniel *kisses* **Meera** *on the forehead*.

Daniel   Rest . . . and maybe stop calling for a bit. It's important you don't take on too much stress, babe. Right, I'm gonna have a shower.

Scene Seven

Daniel's *dreaming. He's in the same position as earlier. The baby in the cot still remains, but not crying this time. We hear the sound of 'Mary Had a Little Lamb' on a baby music box.* **Leon** *enters, he sees the baby but can't hear or see* **Daniel**. **Daniel** *calls out to* **Leon** *repeatedly.* **Leon** *smiles and picks up the baby. He sings the lullaby and exits with the child, while* **Daniel** *fights to break free.*

Scene Eight

Late evening. **Leon**'s *flat. A small room with clothes everywhere.*
Leon *is playing* Call of Duty *online with a boy from Manchester.*
He overhears the boy's mum telling him to get of the computer.

Leon   Your mum said you got to get off the game?

Boy   Yeah, I've been on all day . . .

Leon   That's sad bro, you're a grown man.

Boy   Um, I'm sixteen.

Leon   Well you sound like a grown man that's peak!

Boy   It's peak that I sound like a grown man?

Leon   Yeah, because you're still getting told to get off the
game when you sound like a grown man.

Boy   I mean . . . OK . . . I guess . . .

Leon   You guess . . . fam, stick up for yourself!

Boy   That's my mother.

Leon   I don't care who it is, tell her you ain't getting off the
game you're busy.

Boy   You can disrespect your mother like that.

Leon   I disrespect you and your mum, my guy, now tell her
you ain't getting of the game we're doing shit.

Boy   Fuck you.

Leon (*laughs*)   Ah listen to you, you're mad you gottta come
off the game because you gotta get ready for school
tomorrow . . .

Boy   There's no school tomorrow it's bank holiday,
dickhead . . . you can't keep track of shit.

Leon   Your mum can't keep track of you, that's why you
gotta come off the game . . . plus I don't go school waste
yute, man a big man . . .

Door knocks. **Leon** *ends the game.*

Bless up Likkle man. Yooo . . . who is it?

Daniel   Your dad!

Opens the door. **Daniel** *enters.*

Leon   Fool! What you tellin' me?

Daniel   Nuttin. Man walked through the door n' mumsy was like 'tell Leon not to leave his dutty hat pon mi table!'

Daniel *gives* **Leon** *his hat.*

Leon   Shit, oh yeah.

Daniel   Wagwan?

Leon   Nothing, was just chatting shit on Black Ops.

Daniel   My man lives on that game.

Leon   Fam, after eight hours of, 'can I help you sir', 'sorry no size seven in stock', 'nah but you can order online', man needs a release, bro.

Daniel   Come on . . .

Leon   There's some special fried rice and ribs in there if you want some.

Daniel   Decent.

Leon   Don't box it off though.

Daniel   How you tell a man not to box it off, when you leave bare crumbs.

Leon   Shut up! Just eat what you want.

Daniel *eats what's left.*

Daniel   Tell my man shut up! – Man called it 'Gang Signs and Prayer' yah na.

Leon   Huh?

Daniel   Stormzy . . . how you gonna call your album 'Gang Signs and Prayer', like are you a road man or a church yout . . .

Leon   Both, innit.

Daniel   Negative . . . you can't be both.

Leon   Why?

Daniel   Why?

Leon   Yeah, why?

Daniel   You think God's sayin' 'yeah bless up for the prayers n' dat but can you move these packs real quick'?

Leon   Bro, you sound clever to somebody stupid. You're still active, relax yourself.

Daniel   Says who?

Leon   What I'm dumb, yeah? Exactly! You're still out here, you believe in God and go Uni, you can be whatever you want.

Daniel   Ain't the same, I'm doing this to feed da fam *while* I'm *at* Uni.

Leon   N' before you *went* Uni.

Daniel   You're missing the point.

Leon   Am I though.

Daniel   Big facts! Anyway, that's the quickest way to the sunken place, no idea who you are with fame and money – oi put *Street Fighter* on – you get what I'm saying though, you got to know who you are in this life because you will find yourself loose in the streets real quick, my bruda.

Pause. **Leon** *loads up* Street Fighter *game. They begin to play as they talk.*

Leon   It's just the name of an album bro, bare hatin', shit ain't that serious.

Daniel Yeah, that's what people say but you got to think of the yutes and what message my man's sending out to them.

Leon Makes no sense. There are criminals who believe in God, there are bisexual men and women and there are racists who love their family, people are different bro, so allow man with the GCSE lecture.

Daniel Exactly and those are some confused and lost people.

Leon And what are you?

Daniel Meaning?

Leon What, you ain't confused?

Daniel Man's woke, innit – you're dead at this game –

Leon I'm warming still – if you were woke you'd know you're chatting shit, bro.

Daniel How?

Leon I told you people are different things, you for example have a yute on the way and you ain't got your shit together.

Daniel Oi, don't chat shit.

Leon See how man's lecturing but can't look himself.

Daniel My life's set.

Leon What Muslim girlfriend, who's pregnant, her family won't accept you and she's living at your mum's, yeah you're levelling still.

Daniel Oi, big man, don't chat shit!

Leon Emotional.

Daniel You work in a shop serving people you hate, can't really chat to man right now.

Leon My bills are paid.

Daniel   Yeah but –

Leon   I said my bills are paid.

Daniel   Yeah but where are you going? Anytime I come here it's computer and Chinese – or you *say* you're out linking gyal but I don't see no gyal inside here with you, no wifey!

Leon   Do you live here?

Daniel   Nop . . .

Leon   Well then sekkle yourself –

Daniel   I know you, that's enough.

Leon   How? You ain't even about like that. When you're bored or when Meera's out you holla . . . but since Meera got pregnant and is living at your's, I can't see you, fam!

Daniel   Hold on, hold on, hold on. What you talking about?

Leon   Say nuttin, innit.

Daniel *stands.*

Daniel   Listen, just because man's glowed up and man's life's changed n' shit / don't try –

Leon   See, this is what I'm talking about! You got a little set up and forgot about the mandem . . . You know, I weren't gonna say nothing, but you been dealing with a lot of the mandem on some funny ting lately.

Daniel   Oh, so you lot been chattin', man, yeah, who's saying / what then?

Leon   I'm just saying –

Daniel   What! What you saying?

Leon   Oi, whose yard are you shouting in . . . don't run up your mouth and violate pussy / coz I *will* tump you in your mouth . . .

Daniel   Or what! . . . what!

Daniel *squares up to* **Leon**.

Leon   What, are you mad! You better put your hand on that pregnant fucking terrorist before you try move to man.

Daniel *punches* **Leon**, *the two begin an intense scuffle, knocking over tables and cups.* **Leon** *is stronger, he gets the better of* **Daniel** *and is on top of* **Daniel** *with his hands firmly around his neck.*

Pause. **Leon** *passionately kisses* **Daniel** *on the lips.* **Daniel** *instinctively struggles, breaks free, scurries and is now stood glaring wide eyed at* **Leon**.

Daniel   What the fuck you are doing, are you fucking mad!

Daniel *runs out.*

Leon *slowly gets up, picking up the tables and cups then slumps on the sofa.*

Act Two

Scene One

Evening. Living room. **Meera** *is tidying whilst singing.* **Daniel** *comes in with bags, he's been clothes shopping for the baby.*

Daniel   Yo babes, you seen my mum?

Meera   Food shopping.

Daniel   Cool.

Meera   You sure you got enough bags?

Daniel (*excited*)   Look, look what I got.

Daniel *goes through a sequence of showing* **Meera** *a selection of baby trainers, caps, clothes and blankets.*

Daniel   Look at these Jordans, mad innit, and I got these cute hats and also look . . .

Reveals a designer baby jacket from the bag.

Won't fit her straight away but she'll grow –

Meera   Yeah, it's nice.

Daniel   What . . . just nice?

Meera   Yeah, it's cute.

Daniel   I hear you saying it's cute, but your face is push up like to say – look I'll take them back / if you –

Meera   Where did you get the money to buy all that?

Daniel (*beat*)   Student loan.

Meera   Student loan, right!

Daniel   Yeah, I been saving it / because I knew –

Meera *reveals* **Daniel**'s *bank statement.*

Meera   Then what is this.

Daniel   What's that?

Meera   Your bank statement, you spent that months ago.

Daniel   Why you going through my shit?

Daniel *snatches bank statement.*

Meera   I didn't have to go through your shit, I'm tidying up.

Look I'm grateful, I really am and it's nice stuff but tell me you ain't doing that shit again?

Daniel   I told you –

Meera   I know what you told me but tell me the truth.

Daniel   It is the truth!

Meera   Then why don't I believe you? I told you I'm not bringing up no child here if you're still on that.

Daniel   And I told you I've stopped! Anyway, you didn't mind before . . . when I was spending P on you, and now you got a set of fucking morals you think you can tell man what to do . . . Look what I've done for you. You live here because of me. Your family didn't want you and I made sure you were looked after, so before you start dishing out orders on man look at what the fuck I'm doing for you –

Patricia *enters.*

Patricia   Oi, what is going on inside 'ere?

Pause.

Patricia   Meera, go downstairs . . .

Meera   I'm so sorry –

Patricia   I'm not going to repeat myself.

Meera *goes.*

Patricia   Whose house is this?

Daniel   Let me explain.

Patricia   Mi never ask yuh fi explain nuttin, mi ask yuh a question.

Now, whose house is this?

Daniel   Yours.

Patricia   Dat's right. Don't let mi catch you tarkin dat rubbish about 'why she live here' and 'what yuh done fi her', because di last time I check, this house in *my* name.

Daniel   Why you listening / to our conversation?

Patricia   Nah boda ask mi why mi listening to anything in my own house and I don't want to 'ear you raising yu voice to her like dat full stop.

Deena *comes running up the stairs and bursts in with excitement dancing.*

Deena   Mum, Mum, Mum, guess who's –

Patricia   Not right now Deena, I'm trying to sort out –

Deena   Cool but –

Patricia   I said not right now! I can't do two things at once and I'm trying fi sort out these two inside 'ere.

Deena *is shocked.*

Deena   Do you know what, forget it!

Deena *storms off.*

Patricia   Excuse me! What's di matter wid everyone inside here. Mi have your sister upset every two second for God knows what and then yuh two are fighting whenever mi turn mi back. I just want some bloody peace and quiet inna mi house! Is that too much to ask for? Now what's dis rubbish you tarkin to Meera?

Daniel   We were just talking and then –

Patricia   Then talk! Now is not di time to be shouting at her, giving the gyal all kinds of stress. Listen, whatever yawl arguing about is none of my business, but I'm nobody's fool, but yuh can't do things for people outta the kindness of yuh heart and throw it back in their face when you na like what yuh hear, do I make myself clear?

Daniel   Yes, Mum.

Meera and **Patricia** *exit.* **Daniel** *takes a seat. Deep breath.*

Scene Two

Leon's *flat. A rainy late evening.* **Leon** *is tidying, playing grime music. Door knocking.* **Leon** *turns the music off, looks through the peep hole and opens the door.*

Daniel   Can I holla at you real quick?

Leon (*hesitant*)   Yeah cool.

Daniel *enters.* **Leon** *sits. Apart from the sound of the rain it's silent.*

Daniel   I been outside three hours trying to think what I was gonna say when I come here.

Leon   Listen bro –

Daniel   Let me talk . . . what the fuck, fam! Yo, real early man ain't no eeddiat you know. Trust me, I'm telling you man ain't no eediat! I thought to come back, lick off man's door and do you suttin. But then I thought nah that's Leon. My guy . . . Man vomited for hours. Just kept retching. Like I had something inside of me, inside my veins or some shit. What did you do to me? Why would you do that to me and what drove you to do that to man? Like what was going through your mind? I wanted to kill you. I felt violated . . . and man ain't into taking no violations cuz (*Pause.*) but that moment you kissed me . . . I've never felt so alive . . . it was like I was flying . . . and I've gone back and forth and back and forth over and over, pissed with myself for the way you made me feel. Like what the fuck is wrong with me, because man ain't gay, you feel me, and all I can think about is what is that, like what was that feeling, that's what's fucking with my head.

Daniel *sits. Pause.*

Daniel   What you aint's got nuttin to say, nah?

Leon *sits next to* **Daniel**.

Leon   Fam, I'm sorry.

Pause.

Daniel *puts his hand on top of* **Leon**'s. *An offer.* **Leon**, *momentarily surprised, registers this. Their eyes meet. We feel the electricity between the two. Slowly* **Daniel** *leans in, stopping within an inch of* **Leon**'s *nose. They stare.* **Daniel** *gently pecks* **Leon** *on the lips. Then leans away. The two in unison then slowly lean in sharing a passionate kiss.*

Fade to black.

Scene Three

Daniel's *dreaming. He has one arm released from the chains. A Quran recitation playing.* **Meera** *enters holding a Quran to her chest. He can see her but she makes no eye contact. She begins circling him several times.* **Daniel**, *confused, watches and reaches out to her as she exits.*

Scene Four

Late afternoon. **Daniel**'s *bedroom. Tidy and minimal. A double bed with a TV, wardrobe and chest of drawers.* **Meera** *is laying down on the bed looking at baby names.* **Daniel** *is on his phone sat on the floor.*

Meera   OK, so I've made a list of potential names . . . so the first one is Serah?

Daniel   Nah.

Meera   Isla?

Daniel   No.

Meera   Bella?

Daniel   Nop.

Meera   Mia?

Daniel   Maybe.

Meera   Sienna?

Daniel   Nah.

Meera *realizing* **Daniel**'s *not really listening.*

Meera   Boris?

Daniel   Could do.

Pause.

Meera   You're not even listening to me, are you?

Daniel   Course I am.

Meera   You heard what I just said?

Daniel   Yeah.

Meera   What did I just say then?

Daniel   I heard you!

Meera   Go on, what did I just say?

Daniel   I heard you, babe.

Meera   What did I say?

Daniel (*beat*)   OK, I never heard you!

Meera   Daniel!

Daniel   Alright go, I'm listening.

Meera   Tokyo.

Daniel   You mad?

Meera   Just checking. Aalimah?

Daniel   Maybe.

Meera   Aarifah

Daniel   It's OK, but nah.

Meera   Badriya

Daniel   Mm possibly.

Meera   Jabirah

Daniel   Those last few Muslim names?

Meera   Yep, problem?

Daniel   Obviously not.

Meera   Good. Then I had, Harper, Ava, Siya, Nevaeh/ and Taylor.

Daniel   Nevaeh, I like that.

Meera   It's heaven backwards.

Daniel   Yeah, it's cool.

Meera   – And the last one I had was Cookie?

Daniel   What as in the biscuit?

Meera   Nah as in the animal, course the biscuit, means sweet.

Daniel   Yeah . . . that's not happening, that's a straight application for bullying, babes and . . .

Daniel *puts his head to* **Meera***'s stomach to talk to the baby.*

Daniel   We don't wanna bully you do we huh?

Now listen up, let's get a few things sorted before you land.

Meera   Fool, get off . . .

Daniel   Shh, I'm talking to my princess. You gotta talk to the yute from early, ya nah. Now first things first. Chill with the contouring . . .

Meera *laughs.*

Daniel   Instagram is for eediyats . . . and know you were beautiful before he tells you, you understand? . . . some people ain't gonna like you but nah boda wid dem. Make sure you call your grandma and don't try bring no wasteman to my doorstep, you get me?

Meera (*laughs*)   Especially if his name's Leon . . .

Daniel   What you saying that for?

Meera   What?

Daniel   What you bringing up Leon for?

Meera   I'm joking.

Daniel   I said I don't wanna hear his name again, you hear me?

Meera   I don't know who you think you're talking to . . .

Daniel   Talking to you.

Meera   Listen, don't get mad at because you two fell out. If you don't wanna talk about it then fine but watch how you're talking to me.

Daniel   Listen, I'm . . . sorry I'm grumpy, innit.

Meera   Well come here, I know how to make you feel better.

Meera *attempts to be intimate with* **Daniel**. **Daniel** *pulls away.*

Meera   What's the matter?

Daniel   Nothing.

Pause.

Meera   Listen, I'm pregnant, I'm not sick.

Daniel   Yeah, I know.

Meera   Then what's the matter? You clearly don't wanna have sex with me, do you? You move away, pretend you're asleep or find some dumb excuse, I'm not stupid! Listen, I'm horny and I know what your sex drive is – was like. So, what's the problem? You sleeping with someone else?

Daniel   Ah don't chat –

Meera   Then what is it? Because I ain't getting it so someone else must be.

Daniel   Ah you're –

Meera   I'm what? What, you don't find me attractive no more?

Because I only handle so much fucking rejection.

Daniel *leaves without acknowledging* **Meera**. *She sits on the bed crying heavily.*

Scene Five

Late evening. **Leon***'s room.* **Daniel** *and* **Leon** *listening to Fredo, Stay Flee Get Lizzy, 'Ay Caramba'. The two dance throughout and ad lib.* **Both** *begin to sing together.*

Daniel *begins the chorus, aiming it at* **Leon***, the two are locked in smiling.*

Daniel *then jokingly whines his hips towards* **Leon***.*

But I'm missing my sales when she is whining them hips!!!

And the two burst out laughing, hugging each other. **Daniel** *looks up at* **Leon***.*

Daniel   I love the way you feel.

Pause.

Oi, when did you first clock that, you know . . .

Leon *breaks away from* **Daniel** *turning the music off.*

Leon   When man was in primary school, think like six or seven.

Daniel   Rah, bare early.

Leon   Yeah, I didn't know what it was. I was confused, fam. Then when man got older obviously everyone's chattin' about banging girls and dat, but I knew I was a different.

Daniel   Hold on, you've banged bare tings.

Leon   Yeah? Trust me, it's not that simple. I've only troubled a couple tings still.

Daniel   Nah you're gassing, there was bare times man drew tings and linked them –

Leon   Yeah, but mostly to try force myself away from how I felt.

I backed out last minute bare times.

Daniel   Hold on what about –

Leon   Listen! There's been a couple tings here and there, yes, but I not gonna lie, man, ain't feeling gyal dem like that bare times bro. Think about it, what ting do you really know personally that I've banged? Most of them man had to make up and the others were actually dates with guys out the ends. I say dates, mostly back to their yard or I'd go to these masquerade mask parties, so man won't get clocked.

I've had to make sure my ting pattern up properly from early. No one round here knows apart from you.

Daniel   What you ain't told no one?

Leon   Like who, you?

Daniel   Not gonna lie if you had told man –

Leon   What, what would you have said if I had told you?

Daniel (*beat*)   I don't know. I mean it's you so . . . but honestly I don't know. Do you remember your first / time you . . .

Leon   How you feeling about Meera and –

Daniel   Don't try change the subject bare times bro . . . do you remember your first time?

Pause.

Leon   Thought we said we weren't gonna talk about it?

Daniel   Well, now I wanna know.

Leon   I don't even know what we are doing here, you feel me? I mean this is fun, trust me bro it is, but –

Daniel   But what? I've got a wifey and a yout on the way? Yeah, I know! Don't you think that's in man's head constantly, but I can't deny the way man's feeling.

Leon   I hear you . . . it's confusing, innit . . . you know what everyone says you should be but your brain and body is like, nah this is who you are. I could only pretend to myself for so long, so now I accept it, this is me. My counsellor said it's not a sustainable lifestyle to say nuttin but man ain't got no other choice. I've been to gay bars out of London, it's been fun but there ain't no black people to connect wid. You don't see a black man from the bits openly gay, do you . . .? Well I ain't . . . I just see white men holding hands . . . or if they are black they're acting like they wanna be a rasclat woman. Man ain't camp, you get me, ain't got no girls as my best friend and I can knock most man out clean, you get me. So, think how many others there are like me, hiding in the shadows, operating in the night like foxes, for fear of rejection and a life of ridicule. I've worked too hard to gain my respect only for it to be taken from me because of something I can't control. I said to my counsellor, does he reckon people are born gay and my man said, 'to say we are fully anything is a simplistic statement'. I thought about what he said, hard, and I know with some people there may be shifts but there's categorically zero shifts in me because without doubt I consistently, twenty-four hours a day, like men.

Pause.

Daniel (*playfully*)   Rahhhh, so you been clocking man from early then, yeah?

Pause.

Leon   Shut up. Mam didn't think you were gay.

Daniel   I'm not gay.

Leon   Then, what you been doing in my bed.

Daniel   Bro, I might be confused but man ain't gay!

Leon   Then go be confused somewhere else. This ain't no free trial, ya nah!

Daniel   Woah, woah, woah, woah, woah, hold on . . . I'm just . . . you know . . . it's the word '*gay*' . . . you feel me . . . gets man a bit shook still.

Leon   It's just a word, fam. I don't know what you are or not.

I like spending time with you that's all I know.

Daniel   Yeah, cool cool.

Pause. **Leon** *looks at* **Daniel**.

Leon   Go home, Daniel.

Daniel   What?

Leon   Go home!

Daniel   Why you saying –

Leon   What you doing here? What you gonna do? Tell Meera that you're leaving her coz you're flexing with Leon now. Exactly! You ain't built like that, so when I tell you to go home don't act like you really wanna be here.

Daniel I do really wanna be here.

Leon Why?

Daniel Why?

Leon Yeah why? You can't answer, can you?

Daniel This is all new for me. What? Do you want to me to say yeah I've got all this figured out in my fucking head, that I know exactly what I'm feeling and what this is? Then no I ain't but it's still me, your boy.

Leon And I ain't denying that, I'm just saying man ain't no figuring out situation.

Daniel Look, all I know is I wanna be here with you, I don't know how that plays out.

Leon Well bro, listen to me on a real ting. It's cool you don't know what you're feeling . . . this could be some experimental ting.

Beat.

Listen, I don't want you to do or make some off-the-cuff choice when you ain't sure.

Daniel And what do you want?

Leon Doesn't matter what I want.

Daniel Nah, come on, what do you want?

Leon That's not the point.

Daniel It is. Look this feels more right to me than anything and I'm not gonna lie it's got man shook, so if this is what I am, whatever that means then I wanna know what you're sayin'?

Leon Yeah?

Daniel Yeah?

Leon   Alright . . . then I want you. There, I said it. If I could have it my way I'd want you, and that sounds bare selfish hearing myself even say that but that's the truth.

Pause.

Daniel   I don't even know how this would work . . .

Leon   Exactly. I mean what would you tell Meera . . .

Daniel   I don't know, but it ain't gonna keep me from being a dad, I know that.

Leon   Good. Let me tell you it never works out how we think it's gonna work, you know. I seen it. You see how you'd walk around here and draw a ting. Imagine you couldn't do that, coz man can't do that round here. If anyone round here knew, cuz, it's wrap for you. No family, no mandem . . . you're done out 'ere. Now I ain't got no mum, no sister, no girlfriend, no family but you do. So you think about that and don't allow this moment to cloud your judgement. Do you hear me?

Daniel   I hear you.

Beat.

I wanna be with you.

Black.

Scene Six

Late evening. Outside **Leon***'s flat.* **Meera** *is trying to figure out which door is* **Leon***'s.* **Leon** *smoking a zoot, returns, frightening* **Meera***.*

Leon   Meera?

Meera   Fuck, you frightened me –

Leon   Sorry, you OK?

Leon *puts the zoot out.*

Meera   Yeah, just let me get my breath back . . . I couldn't work out which number was yours.

Leon   It's cool, what you doing here . . . you alright?

Meera   Yeah, I'm good, not too long to go now.

Leon   Cool.

Meera   Actually, I ain't good. I came here to speak to you about something private.

Leon   OK cool, erm I'd say come up but the lift ain't working.

Meera   Here's fine.

They sit on the wall. Silence.

Meera   Sooo . . .

Leon   So, what . . .

Meera   Ain't you gonna say nothing?

Leon   Say nothing about what? You said you came here to talk to me.

Meera   You two still not speaking?

Leon   Is that what he told you?

Meera   Uh huh . . .

Leon (*beat*)   Meera, how come you ain't never liked me?

Meera   Says who?

Leon   Says the way you act when I'm about.

Meera   I don't really know what to say.

Leon   Cool.

Meera   Nah I mean – look I used to think you were a bad influence on him but then I realised that . . . that was just him. You a hard one to figure out. So, aloof, so I guess when I can't figure someone out I get kinda quiet around them, but nah you're cool, you weirdo.

Beat.

Who do you live here with anyway?

Leon   Meera, why'd you come here?

Meera (*beat*)   Well I know, innit.

Leon (*surprised*)   Huh?

Meera   And don't say nothing for a second and please don't even bother with the dumb look on your face because it will just make this more drawn out than it needs to be. I'm not here to judge or blame. This is about me and this child. I'm not mad at you, I'm just a bit confused. I'm gonna need to hear your side. This is my life at the end of the day.

Leon   I can't believe he told you.

Meera   Ah so there is something, fuck me you didn't take long to crack did you? You're as dumb as he is, so come on, speak up, who is she?

Leon   Who is sh – what you talking about?

Meera   Don't chat shit. I know Daniel's been banging someone tramp.

Leon   Oh – nah I don't know nothing about that!

Meera   You just said you couldn't / believe he told me.

Leon   I thought / you were

Meera   What?

Leon (*turning away*)   Ah noth – forget it it's long.

Meera *grabs* **Leon**'*s jacket.*

Meera   No what?

Leon   Meera, let go of me.

Meera   You see the thing about you is you ain't got no one so all you care about is your fucking self. If you settled down and found someone you'd then understand. Now, I know deep down you know better, so why don't you do better and tell me the truth.

Leon   I'm telling you the truth, I don't know nothing about no girl, he told you we don't even talk anyway so how would I know? My life doesn't revolve around him, you know.

Meera   That's the thing, yes it does! It's fine. You look me in my face and you keep them secrets . . . lay with your conscience when you sleep.

Leon   Oh my – I'm telling you the truth!

Meera   So, what did you think I was talking about?!

Pause.

Leon   It's not for me to tell you.

Meera   You know what, Leon, bye!

Meera *goes.*

Leon   Meera, I'm sorry.

Meera   I know . . . sorry is exactly what you are.

She goes.

Scene Seven

Daniel's *dreaming. He is crying. We can hear 'Oh Freedom' by The Golden Gospel Singers. Daniel easily releases himself from the chains. He walks forward and kneels in the prayer position. He prays rocking back and forth.*

Black out.

Scene Eight

Late afternoon. Kitchen. **Patricia** *is putting food away in the cupboards. She is singing the gospel song 'I Need You Now' by Smokie Norful.*

Daniel *enters.*

Daniel   Mum, where's Meera and Deena?

Patricia   Daniel, lard God yuh frighten mi! Where yuh been? Yuh been gone fi two days and Meera is worried sick.

Daniel   Where are they?

Patricia   Gone out I think.

Daniel   Sit down, Mum.

Patricia   I said where yuh been and why yuh inna dem same smelly clothes, Daniel? Go upstairs, take a shower before I get vex with you.

Daniel   Sit down, Mum.

Patricia   You can't run around di place as yuh please and nah let anyone know where yuh is.

Daniel   I SAID SIT DOWN, MUM!

Patricia *startled sits. Pause.*

Patricia   Daniel?

Daniel   Please, Mum. I need to talk to you . . . I . . .

Patricia (*beat*)   What is it, son.

Daniel   I need you to listen . . . I need . . .

Patricia (*beat*)   Speak son. Mi nah like to see yuh like dis yah nah. Yuh look all shook up like yuh seen a ghost . . . Now you know yuh mudda will always listen so let it out.

Pause.

Patricia   Daniel . . .

Daniel   How long have we been living here, Mum . . . Hm? Loud music, good food, I mean you can smell the food down the balcony. Church every Sunday . . . nobody can't tell us nothing, innit Ma. 'I mean that family ain't got a dad but boi don't try a ting wid them, ya nah'. That's how they see us round here, Mum, innit . . . strong! How do they see me . . . loudmouth, nah nah womaniser, nah nah nah, trouble maker, innit.

But who am I really, Mum, because I don't know anymore. The last two nights I've slept in that park thinking about how I was gonna come to talk to you. What I was going to say to you. I went back and forth a thousand times, so I'm going to need you to listen to me, Mum, and not just the words I'm saying but the pain it's coming from, because this ain't easy. Remember I love you and I'm still your son. I've been having a relationship with a man. I like men.

Patricia *kisses her teeth and continues putting the shopping away.*

Daniel   I'm serious, Mum! This isn't a choice or phase, it's a realisation that I've been living a lie my entire life. I'm sorry, Mum.

A very long silence.

Mum? . . . Mum?

Daniel *fidgets, unsure what to do with himself. A silence.*

Daniel   You're not gonna say nothing?

A silence . . . and then . . .

Patricia   Go upstairs and bring yuh dutty clothes down fi wash, there's no cleaner inside here. I'm a start cook up something.

Daniel   Mum, I'm ga –

Patricia *turns and fiercely throws a frozen pack of peas at him which hit him on his side.*

Patricia   SHUT UP! Nah boda disrespect me inside my house, yuh understand!!!

Daniel   Mum, I'm scared, and I really need you to – I'm praying to God/ to guide me.

Patricia   How dare yuh mention God wid dis nonsense yuh talking?

What yuh mean yuh been having a relationship with man. You got some blasted nerve fi come inside of mi house chatting some devil shit. Yuh have a woman who loves yuh and a daughter pon di way and yuh dere, mixing wid dem devil people dem. The Bible says it clear in Leviticus 18.22 'Thou shalt not lie with mankind: as with womankind: it is abomination' . . . and again in Leviticus 20.13 – look at me when I'm talking to yuh . . . if a man lies wid a male as he lies wid a woman, both of dem have committed an abomination. 'They shall surely be put to death; their blood shall be upon them.' God's punishment for mixing / with dem devil worshippers.

Daniel   You're not lis –

Patricia   Shut yuh mouth! I tank God your farda's not alive to hear dis, it would a send him to an early grave.

Daniel   Yuh said I could always tell yuh anything.

Patricia   Mi nah waan here dis bloodclat disrespect!

Daniel   Mum, this isn't a choice!

Patricia   Of course it's a choice . . . it's wrong, yuh hear me, it's wrong. Who yuh been hanging around with, huh? What people yuh been mixing wid that come and corrupt yuh mind?

Daniel   Why has it got to be that someone's corrupted my mind?

Patricia   Because yuh can't just change up your brain like that.

Daniel   People change all the time. We evolve, Mum.

Patricia   Yes, in life but not in yuh sexual preference.

Daniel   Says who?

Patricia   Says life, and I've been around longer then yuh to know how dis ting works.

Daniel   Yes, you have been around longer than me, but you don't know how every human being works.

Patricia   *You* are not a gay . . . look at me at me when I'm talking to yuh . . . yuh understand?

Pause.

Daniel   Then, why do I feel –

Patricia   Because yuh confused . . . Now, who poisoned yuh mind wid dis wickedness?

Daniel   It's not wickedness / it's natural.

Patricia   Stop di rubbish and tell me who been mixin' wid?

Daniel   Doesn't matter.

Patricia   I said who you been mixin' wid!

Daniel   I got my own mind –

Patricia   Daniel! / Dis is yuh mudda speaking – yes it is important, because I'm di one that bring yuh up – help! What kinda help? Yuh should of thought about that before. Now stop yuh noise and tell me who – you're not gonna talk over me, yuh understand . . . yuh understand . . . I said yuh understand?!

Daniel   I told you it's not important . . . what's important is that I'm here asking for help and if you don't wanna help me then fine I'll do this alone no problem . . . no, I won't stop my noise, Mum, I'm not a kid, I'm a grown man and I'm allowed to speak.

Patricia *slaps* **Daniel** *across the face.*

Patricia   Now, who you been mixin' wid?

Pause.

Patricia   Nah let mi talk twice inside 'ere yu nah . . .

Daniel   Look, it doesn't matter who it is, that's who I am, Mum and you're gonna have to accept / that.

Patricia   Mi? I will never accept that. Yuh doing dis to hurt mi, aren't yuh? What have I done to yuh to deserve dis?

What have I done to yuh for yuh fi bring such shame on our family name. I cook, clean, bring yuh and your sister up by myself, work every hour God send and dis is what I get.

Oh lord God, please tell me dis ain't so. My son is not a gay. I never raised my son to be that way, to lay down with no man and do all kinda nastiness. Yuh say yuh praying for God to guide yuh, yuh better pray him wash dis ting /outta you!

Daniel   I don't know why I feel the way I do or why this happened to me but I'm gonna have to deal with it. You brought us up to treat people equally, you instilled morals in us, I'm the same person you raised to always remember that we are all God's children and I'm the same person you knew right before I told you this. God loves us all regardless of our sin, those are your words you've told us all for the last twenty odd years right, Ma? Now all of sudden it's on your doorstep you can't see no love. Then why are you going to church, Ma, if you can't even attempt to practice what you preach?

Deena *appears at the door.*

Deena   He's right, Mum.

Daniel   Deena . . .

Pause.

Patricia   Deena . . . I thought yuh were out, go upstairs.

Daniel   Deena –

Deena (*to* **Daniel**)   Now, *you* stop!

Sorry, Mum, but this is not a go upstairs Deena moment. You taught us to love and treat people equally and then now, when our own flesh and blood comes in crisis, we close our door?

Patricia   What? It's not di same. Now I told yuh / to go upstairs.

Deena   Why isn't it? Because it's uncomfortable, because it's here in our house?

Patricia Yuh don't understand.

Deena Listen, I may be the youngest in here and you might think I don't know anything but that's still Daniel as far as I'm concerned, whether I agree with it or not and we're all part of the living garment of God despite our shortcomings. What, I'm gonna turn my back on him?

Patricia What a waste of a man. How is he supposed to raise a child when him a mix up in dis nastiness?

Deena Mum, you sound ignorant.

Patricia Watch yuh mouth, child!

Deena It's true, Mum! You've lectured us for years about how Jesus ate with prostitutes, Jesus ate with the tax collectors, Jesus ate with the sick. Then in his time of need, when he most needs you, you're gonna turn your back? In life we are either heading into a storm, in the body of a storm or just coming out a storm, Mum and right now we're in one.

Daniel Mum, you're angry because you're afraid, but I'm afraid too.

Daniel *attempts to hug* **Patricia**. *She refuses.*

Daniel I'm afraid too!

Patricia You disgust mi. I'm ashamed to say yuh come out of mi.

Deena Mum!

Patricia I SAID WATCH YOU MOUT!

Deena *is silenced.*

Patricia Now I want you outta this house right now!

Daniel What – you're chucking –

Patricia Mi not inna no conversation, I want you out of this house right now!

Daniel *picks up his coat. Goes to leave then suddenly stops at the door.*

Daniel   Mum, you're being –

Patricia   I SAID GET OUT!

Daniel *goes. The air is still as* **Patricia** *continues putting her shopping into the cupboards.*

Deena   Who are you, Mum? . . . Mum, you can ignore me all you want but how can you justify throwing him out!

Patricia   Excuse mi! I don't have to justify anything to anybody inside 'ere and before you start getting ideas about defending that kinda nastiness I'd think again.

Deena   I know you think I don't know nuffin, but I'm tellin' you you're living in the dark ages . . . you're from a different generation where things were different but that doesn't –

Patricia   So you think that kinda nasty behaviour is right?

Deena   It's not about –

Patricia   Answer de question. Do you think that a man laying down with another man is right?

Deena   It's not wrong or right, it's how people are born.

Patricia   Born, so how 'im big twenty-three and only now 'im a stand up in mi face talking all this rubbish if it's how 'im born.

Why 'im never come to mi years ago talking this stupidness eh? . . . because nobody is born that way. It's dis nasty circles thata fool up him brain and I'm not going to have this nonsense inside my house. Mi kno it's dem English bwoy dat fool up im head ya nah.

Deena   Well I don't agree.

Patricia   Mi never raise yuh fi defend dis kinda behaviour.

Deena   He's the only man I have left in my life to look up to . . . and you're kicking him out because he had the guts to come to you and speak his truth. So you're tellin' me Daniel goes against the Bible and you kick him out but Meera goes against the Quran but you let her live here, why, because it's not your religious book? It's hypocr –

Patricia   THAT'S ENOUGH! I don't know who put a battery inna yuh back for yuh fi come inside here flaring up flaring up. Now, I'm not going down dis road with –

Deena   Well, if he can't live here I'm moving out.

Patricia   Come again?

Deena   I said if Daniel can't live here then I can't live here.

Patricia   And go where, where yuh a go?

Deena   Get my own place

Patricia   Eh eh. And whose money yuh a go use fi get yuh place?

Deena   I got a new job.

Patricia   Wha – which job?

Deena   The J.P. Morgan job.

Patricia   So why yuh never tell me?

Deena   I've tried but you never listen to me, Mum!

Patricia   Mi never li – You better help me put away these things, yuh hear?

Deena   I mean it, if he goes I go.

Patricia   I'm not going to be blackmailed inside my house!

Deena   It's not black –

Patricia   I SAID IM NOT GOING TO BE BLACKMAILED INISDE MY HOUSE! What have I sacrificed mi life for when yuh and that bwoy give mi this big level of disrespect.

Now, no boda answer mi back and pick up yuh backside and put away de rest of de shopping yuh understand!

Deena *regroups and does as she's told.*

Act Three

Scene One

Leon's *living room.* **Leon** *is listening to 'Wiley Flow' by Stormzy, putting his football gear in the wash.* **Daniel**'s *knocking at the door.* **Leon** *lets him in.*

Leon   Yo, what you blowing up man's phone for, I was –

Daniel *is pacing the room.*

Daniel   Nah, hold up bro, hear this . . .

Leon *turns the music off.*

(*Beat.*) I told my mum, innit . . .

Leon (*beat*)   What?

Daniel   I dun told you man was serious cuz . . .

Leon   Told her what? What did she say?

Daniel   What do you think she said? Cuss man out, innit obviously, but I feel some mad weight's been lifted off man's shoulders, ya nah, man had bare stress / on the brain.

Leon   What – why didn't you tell man you was –

Daniel   I just needed to do it and get it out.

Leon   Hold on hold on, hold on, hold on bro, nah nah . . . did you tell her about me?

Daniel   Is that all you thinking about . . . you? Man comes here and tell dat and you're / thinking about you?

Leon   Nah, I'm jus sayin –

Daniel   Thought you'd be happy.

Leon   Nah, I am it's just –

Daniel   Doesn't seem like it. Course I didn't tell her about you . . .

Leon   Nah, nah, it's just . . . wish you'd of told me you were gonna do it . . .

Daniel   What difference would it of made? Do you know what it took for me to go tell my mum today? Do you know the fuckrey I had to hear from her and you're asking about you?

Leon   Listen, I'm just saying you didn't tell man you was actually gonna do it.

Beat.

Now I need to know exactly what you said.

Daniel   What you getting all shook for? I told her, she cuss man out and then, then Deena heard and came in –

Leon   Deena heard?

Daniel   Yeah.

Leon   See, this is why you shoulda told man before you –

Daniel   What!

Leon   She's gonna tell her people and – ah forget it you don't understand. People are gonna think it's me.

Daniel   She ain't gonna say nuttin. What you getting all para for? You said if you can have it your way you'd want to be with me, so I make the steps to make that happen and now you on some shook ting.

Leon   But what exactly did –

Daniel   I told her I'm gay! That I like men! That's it. Am I regretting saying it? No! – I don't know. But you're acting like some psycho, calm the fuck down, cuz!

Leon   I'm . . . I'm just . . . I'm just in shock.

Daniel   Imagine how I feel.

Leon   What did Deena say?

Daniel   I feel like all you're thinking about is yourself, I'm not gonna lie.

Leon   Trust me, I i'nt.

Daniel   Well, it kinda feels like it.

Leon   Well, maybe I am, I been hiding this shit for years, so try and understand that I can't have man round here knowing.

Daniel   Fam, I only told my mum.

Leon   And Deena.

Daniel   She walked in – what do you want me to do, sit down and write a plan with you before I do something?

Beat.

This was for us, you know. Not just for myself, so take your selfish head out your ass and recognise that.

Leon   Who you talking to?

Daniel   I'm talking to you, don't think coz man's sweet on you that you're gonna dictate how man runs his life.

Leon   Man i'nt saying 'im gonna dictate your life!

Daniel   Then what you saying then?

Leon   I don't know, let's just slow this shit down for a second.

Pause.

Daniel   What?

Leon   Let's just slow, up innit, you're moving bare fast, tellin' your mum and all that. It's too much too fast, cuz.

Daniel   Hold on, hold on, hold on, you locking man off?

Leon   I ain't sayin' dat, just let's cool off for a sec, innit.

Daniel   What?

Leon   I said let's keep a little fucking distance for a bit, man can't handle all this, cuz!

Daniel   Hold up, so you tell me you wanna be with man, I tell my mum and you're trying to low key lock man off, are you dumb?

Leon   I never told you to tell your mum. Fam, just because you clocked you gay two seconds ago don't get fucking righteous pussyhole.

Daniel *punches* **Leon**. *The two begin to fight,* **Daniel** *is on top but* **Leon** *is too strong and throws* **Daniel** *across the room.* **Daniel** *runs out.*

Scene Two

Leon *is at Footlocker working, sorting out the Nike rack.* **Deena** *walks in and is browsing and suddenly she spots* **Leon**. *She sneaks up behind him pretending to scare him, putting on a manly voice.*

Deena   Oi my yout!

Leon *is momentarily startled.*

Leon   Deena, what you doing here?

Deena   What you doing here?

Leon   Er, I work here.

Deena   Yeah, I can see that, I didn't know you worked here.

Leon   Huh, how? I've worked here two years.

Deena   Is it, I didn't even know what you did to be honest. Come to think of it, I don't think I've seen you outside my mum's.

Leon   Shut up, how can I help you anyway, Deena?

Deena   Nah, just looking to buy a quick Air Forces still.

Leon   Yeah, your creps are dead, I'm not gonna lie.

Deena   Shut up!

Leon   You actually came out your house like that.

Deena   This boy's a dickhead, you know.

Leon   Why you in this branch anyway though, you know there's one by –

Deena   Yeah obviously, but I live a few roads down still.

Leon   Ah, you moved out?

Deena   Yeah, got a little place on Green Lanes.

Leon   Whaaaat! . . . look at yeah, yeah, big gyal yeah, got your likkle place and n' dat yeah . . . big gyal, OK, OK.

Deena   You fool.

Leon   Nah, nah say nuttin.

Deena   What you sayin' anyway, you seen Daniel about?

Leon   Nah, ain't seen him you know.

Deena   What he come check you or nuttin, nah?

Leon   I been kinda busy still, so I ain't even been about like dat.

Deena   When did you last see him?

Leon   It's been a minute still. I ain't spoke to him since . . . you know the little problem but –

Deena   Problem, what problem?

Pause.

Leon   Obviously you'd know, well I just thought you woulda known as you live – well lived in the same house n' dat.

Deena   He told you?

Pause.

Leon   Told me what?

Deena   What you talking about?

Leon   Nah nah, he jus' mentioned he weren't staying at home, 'cause of some argument with your mum but he didn't really go into detail. To be honest, like I said, I got busy and he seem like he needed to sort life stuff out so man just got on with my own shit, you feel me.

Deena   Yeah, so you ain't spoke to him recent recent?

Leon   Nah nah, why what's up?

Deena   Nah nuttin, I been busy with work and sorting my flat out so just thought he'd of been around you. I know Mum and Meera ain't heard from him either.

Leon   Ah OK, nah. So what trainers you looking at, one of these yeah, coz if my manager clocks me standing here talking to you he gonna start chatting shit, also you're fucking up man's commission still.

Deena   Gimme these in a four-n-a-half.

Leon   Beggin, you dun know you ain't no four-n-a-half.

Leon *speaks into the radio.*

Leon   Can I get a five-n-a-half / in the white and crimson.

Deena   I'm a four-n-a-half you waste.

Leon   Nah, furthermore gimme a six-n-a-half.

Deena   Leon!

Leon   Nah, I'm playing, just a four-n-a-half.

Deena   Tell 'em to hurry up, I got shit to do.

Leon   Excuse me?

Deena   Tell 'em to hurry up, man.

Leon   You lucky I'm at work coz man would just put hands-n-feet on you.

Deena   Shut up.

Leon   So what's everyone saying then, how's Mum n' Meera?

Deena   Yeah, they're good. Meera's still staying there, she looks like she's gonna pop any second, boy. I'm going over this week at some point.

Leon   I can imagine, that's good to hear.

Deena   Well, if you hear from Daniel, try link him, innit.

Leon   Yeah, course will do, why?

Deena   Nah, just he seemed to have a lot on his plate when I last spoke to him and I don't think he would say, but I got the feeling he could use a friend, someone that knows him knows him.

Leon   Ah OK, well a baby will do that, new priorities n' dat you know what I mean.

Deena   So he didn't mention anything else?

Leon   Fam, are you Columbo or suttin? I'm at work and you're interrogating man.

Deena   You're his bredrin, innit.

Leon   Do you tell your bredrins every little thing?

Deena   Yeah.

Leon   Do you tell them you're coming here lying about the size of your feet?

Deena   Pagan yout.

Leon   Look, if you wanna tell me suttin, tell me suttin innit, but allow the cryptic questioning.

The radio guy says they are out of size four-n-a-halfs.

Leon   We're out of your size.

Deena   Ah OK.

Leon   Have a look at the crimson Jordans?

Deena   Nah, I'm good.

Leon Ah, you're broke innit, I get it I get it.

Deena What's wrong with you?

Leon Yeah yeah, window shopper. Anyway I gotta get back to work.

Deena Cool, if you hear from him, let me know, yeah?

Leon Course, course, course.

Deena Right, I'm gone.

Leon In a bit, D.

Deena *goes and* **Leon** *gets back to work.*

Scene Three

Leon's *flat.* **Daniel** *and* **Leon** *are intensely dancing to Headie One's 'Both'. Suddenly the music stops. Their eyes meet. Black out.*

Scene Four

Patricia's *living room.* **Meera** *is now nine months pregnant.* **Meera** *is sat while* **Daniel** *is stood by the living room door.*

Meera Nah, nah, let me finish. You wouldn't even touch me. My anxiety was so bad. I went through hell and lost my family for you to turn around and spit in my face . . . but there's something about it not being another woman made me realise that this wasn't something you were doing to me. It wasn't even about me. I felt sorry for you and then I thought fuck that because no one ain't feeling sorry for me. I can't get back what I've lost.

Daniel I want to try put things right / Meera, I want you to know –

Meera You shoulda tried to put things right before you laid down with that man, because you weren't thinking about no one but yourself. Where's my family, where's my family now? I should have avoided you like they told me to. Bad man Daniel. You like men, yeah? Bad man Daniel likes men?

Daniel   I was confused, my head was all over the place, but the main thing is I wanna be here for our daughter and whatever it takes I'll do.

Meera   Listen to this righteous shit.

Daniel   Why you gotta make this so hard? Do you think I wanted this to turn out like this.

Meera   I don't know what you wanted, but it certainly wasn't me.

Daniel   I don't know what I was thinking, I got confused –

Meera   Who confused you –

Daniel   Doesn't matter who, but I realised that shit fucked man's head up but that's not who I am and I know I can't erase what I did to you but all I want is to do whatever I can to be the best dad I can.

Meera   Oh so now you're not gay anymore?

Daniel   What do you think I'm tellin' you!

Pause.

My head got all fucked up and I lost you in the process but I don't expect you to just believe me. I know I can't turn back time . . . but I'm so so sorry, Meera.

Meera   I can't trust you and to be honest a part of me died inside when I heard what you did. I ain't got no one else. You were my best friend and I really wanted us to be a family. I'm lucky Patricia has shown me nothing but love, care and support. My health and this baby are the most important thing and without her I don't know what I would have done.

Meera *breaks down crying*.

Daniel   I'm sorry.

Daniel *comforts* **Meera**.

Daniel   Look, I know I hurt you, I know there's nothing I can do to even begin to erase the pain I've caused but I wanna –

The front door slams.

Patricia   Meera, mi back darlin' . . . It cold out dere yuh nah, how yuh –

She enters the living room seeing **Daniel** *stood watching her. The air is thick and* **Patricia**'s *posture stiffens.* **Daniel** *and* **Patricia** *are staring at each other.* **Meera** *looks on.*

Daniel   Alright, Mum . . .

Pause.

Patricia   Nah boda 'alright Mum' me.

Daniel   Mum please.

Patricia   For yuh to be inna my house must mean yuh washed dat nastiness outta yuh skin . . .

Daniel   I have, Mum.

Patricia (*beat*)   Come again?

Daniel   That's why I'm here. I'm sorry, Mum . . . I know I've brought shame to your doorstep but please forgive me. I allowed people to confuse me and fool up my brain . . . but I've prayed hard . . . harder than I ever have and I promise you that I will never dare to come chat some nonsense in your house again. It's the biggest disrespect and I know it's not right but please please accept my apology and allow me to be the son you have always been proud of.

Patricia's *eyes fill with tears and she breaks down crying.*

Daniel *comforts and hugs her.*

Daniel   Now I don't know what happens next or how we move forward but I know I have work to do and I will do whatever needs to be done.

Meera   You gotta be having a laugh.

Daniel   Meera, please, I'm trying to make this –

Meera   NO! I think my waters just broke.

Daniel   What!

Patricia   Ohh my gawd, Daniel bring the car around. Go, go. Wha' yuh waiting for!!!

Panic ensues. **Daniel** *darts out the front door while* **Patricia** *helps* **Meera** *up and out the front door.*

Scene Five

Daniel*'s dreaming. He and* **Leon** *are slow dancing to Gregory Issac, 'Night Nurse' in* **Leon***'s living room. The two look up at each other. A moment. Lights out.*

Scene Six

A year later. **Patricia***'s kitchen.* **Nevaeh***'s first birthday party. Balloons fill the house.* **Patricia** *is sat reading The Prodigal Son to* **Nevaeh** *as she sleeps.*

Patricia   When he came to his senses, he said, 'How many of my father's hired servants have food to spare, and here I am starving to death! I will set out and go back to my father and say to him: Father, I have sinned against heaven and against you. I am no longer worthy to be called your son; make me like one of your hired servants.' So he got up and went to his fath –

Meera *enters.*

Meera   Hey, Bible study again. I hope you have a Quran in your pocket somewhere.

Patricia   I couldn't read that if I tried, dear.

Meera   Very true.

Patricia   Anyway, the word of God is the Word of God.

Meera   Indeed it is.

Patricia   Yuh alright?

Meera   Yeah of course, I just can't believe she's one already.

Patricia   Well, yuh wait till she's running about and answering you back, then yuh really ah go want to beg, borrow and steal for time fi slow up.

Meera   That's what people keep telling me.

Patricia   Oh dear, I hope I cook enough food, maybe I should put on another pot of something . . .

Meera   Patricia, there's enough food here to feed the street twice over.

Patricia   I hope so, me nah used to cooking for so many mouths anymore yuh know . . . but that is how tings go.

Meera   Deena always pops round.

Patricia   Yes, but it's not di same.

Doorbell goes.

Meera   I'll get it.

Deena *and* **Daniel** *enter. They all greet each other.* **Deena** *has a huge wrapped present in her hand.*

Deena   Where's the birthday girl?

Meera   Oh my gosh, Deena, she's going to be spoilt if you keep buying her all these presents.

Daniel   That's what I keep telling her.

Deena   I can't help it, I have to.

They all go through to the kitchen.

Patricia   Ahhh about time – but wait, Deena, yuh buy that big big present? All these years I've been working in the wrong job. I hope yuh saving yuh riches.

Deena *and* **Patricia** *do a well-rehearsed two step as they great each other.*

Deena   Well hello to you, Mum . . . Suttin smell niiiccce . . .

Daniel   All right, Mum . . . Jeeez, yeah suttin smells *decent* in 'ere, what you cooking?

Daniel *goes to open the pot.*

Patricia   Move yuh hand from di pot, it nah ready yet.

Two seconds yuh been inside here and yuh hand in di pot already. Deena, stir the curry goat for me nah.

Daniel   Where's trouble?

Meera   Sleeping.

Daniel   How you sleeping on your birthday . . .

Daniel *and* **Meera** *go into the front room. He gently kisses* **Nevaeh***'s head.*

Meera   Don't wake her.

Daniel   Nah, I won't. I got some stuff for her.

Meera   Thanks.

Daniel   You good, how's things?

Meera   Yeah OK, you?

Daniel   Yeah good, good, good.

Meera   That's a lot of goods.

Daniel   Nah, nah, I'm cool. How's she been?

Meera   Yeah OK, she shook off that cold. You still taking her Saturday?

Daniel   Yeah, I'll be up about two. My little trouble maker still asleep. She can sleep for England.

Meera   I'm telling you.

Patricia *enters the front room.*

Daniel   Food ready yet, Ma?

Patricia   When it's ready it will appear.

Meera   I'm gonna give Deena a hand.

Meera *goes.* **Daniel** *sits.*

Patricia   Yuh alright?

Daniel   Yeah . . .

Patricia   And you're looking after yourself?

Daniel   As best as I can.

Patricia   That's what mi like fi hear.

Patricia *sits next to* **Daniel**. *They watch* **Nevaeh**.

Patricia   You're doing a great job wid her yuh know . . .

Daniel   Well, I had the best teacher.

Patricia   Too right . . .

Patricia *takes* **Daniel**'s *hand.*

Patricia (*beat*)   I'm proud of yuh and all you've achieved . . .

Pause.

And I'm glad yuh left all that wickedness behind, yuh hear me.

Daniel (*beat*)   I love you, Mum.

He hugs her.

Patricia   Right . . . let mi go and make sure these young ladies haven't mash up mi kitchen.

She goes. **Daniel** *is sat staring and* **Nevaeh**. *Doorbell goes.* **Meera** *opens the door. It's* **Leon** *with a gift. She welcomes him in.*

Patricia   Well, look who it is, di invisible man himself.

Leon   Hi, Mum . . .

Leon *takes off his cap and goes to put it on the table.*

Patricia   Eh, eh, nah boda put yuh dusty hat pon mi table.

Leon *puts it in his pocket.*

Leon   Sorry, Mum!

Patricia   Lard God gimme strength. Mi never know yuh was coming up . . .

Deena   I invited him, Mum. (*To* **Leon**.) What you saying, big head . . .

Leon   I'm not staying long, I'm just passing . . . Oh here's a little something.

He gives **Meera** *the present.*

Meera   Oh.

Deena   Let me guess, trainers, innit.

Leon   Obviously. They might be kinda big but . . .

Meera   I'm sure they're fine. Thanks.

Patricia *and* **Leon** *go into the front room.*

Patricia   Well, look what the cat dragged in . . .

Daniel *is surprised to see* **Leon**. *He sits.*

Daniel   Wagwan . . .

Leon   What you tellin' me . . .

Nevaeh *wakes up.* **Daniel** *attends to her.*

Daniel   Is my little birthday girl awake?

Patricia   Ahh, yes she is . . . let mi sort out the cake fi bring in.

She goes. A moment.

Daniel (*whispering*)   What you doing here, bro?

Leon   What?

Daniel   Bro?

Leon   Deena invited me, innit. What am I gonna say, no?

Daniel   This guy you know.

Leon   Plus, it's an important day for you.

Daniel   I was gonna ask you to come but you was gone when I woke up.

Leon   Yeah, I'm on earlies, I didn't wanna wake you. Listen I get it, if you want man to go –

Daniel   Don't be stupid.

Daniel *looks to the door and then puts his hand on* **Leon***'s leg.*

Daniel   I don't know what I'd do without you . . .

Leon   Anywhere you go I go.

They stare at each other and smile.

Deena (*from off*)   We're bringing the cake through!

Daniel *and* **Leon** *like clockwork both re-adjust and create distance between them.* **Daniel** *picks up* **Nevaeh**.

The rest enter with the cake, singing happy birthday and they all join in. **Daniel** *blows out the candle for* **Nevaeh**. *Black out.*

End of play.

www.ingramcontent.com/pod-product-compliance
Ingram Content Group UK Ltd.
Pitfield, Milton Keynes, MK11 3LW, UK
UKHW020707280225
455688UK00012B/302